Nev's Big Day

by Steve Barlow and Steve Skidmore

Illustrated by Geo Parkin

Today is a big day for Neville.

He's going out bus-spotting.

This is Neville's friend Mick.

Mick is also going bus-spotting.

Neville has asked Mick to take photographs of buses with his instant camera.

Here are some of the things Mick would rather do than go bus-spotting.

Neville's dad runs the biggest Virtual Reality game centre in the entire universe.

Neville has promised to get Mick free tickets.

This is why Mick has agreed to go bus-spotting.